IMPROVING FARMING AND FOOD SCIENCE TO FIGHT CLIMATE CHANGE

by Rachel Kehoe

FOCUS READERS.
NAVIGATOR

WWW.FOCUSREADERS.COM

Copyright © 2023 by Focus Readers®, Lake Elmo, MN 55042. All rights reserved. No part of this book may be reproduced or utilized in any form or by any means without written permission from the publisher.

Focus Readers is distributed by North Star Editions:
sales@northstareditions.com | 888-417-0195

Produced for Focus Readers by Red Line Editorial.

Content Consultant: Peter Lehner, Managing Attorney of the Sustainable Food & Farming Program at Earthjustice, Coauthor of *Farming for Our Future: The Science, Law, and Policy of Climate-Neutral Agriculture*

Photographs ©: Shutterstock Images, cover, 1, 6, 8–9, 10, 14–15, 17, 19, 21, 22–23, 25, 27; Angela Weiss/AFP/Getty Images, 4–5; Red Line Editorial, 13, 29

Library of Congress Cataloging-in-Publication Data
Names: Kehoe, Rachel, author.
Title: Improving farming and food science to fight climate change / by
  Rachel Kehoe.
Description: Lake Elmo, MN : Focus Readers, [2023] | Series: Fighting
  climate change with science | Includes index. | Audience: Grades 4-6
Identifiers: LCCN 2022008869 (print) | LCCN 2022008870 (ebook) | ISBN
  9781637392720 (hardcover) | ISBN 9781637393246 (paperback) | ISBN
  9781637394236 (ebook pdf) | ISBN 9781637393765 (hosted ebook)
Subjects: LCSH: Sustainable farming--Juvenile literature. |
  Agroforestry--Juvenile literature. | Agriculture--Climatic
  factors--Juvenile literature.
Classification: LCC S494.5.S86 K44 2023 (print) | LCC S494.5.S86 (ebook)
  | DDC 634.9/9--dc23/eng/20220309
LC record available at https://lccn.loc.gov/2022008869
LC ebook record available at https://lccn.loc.gov/2022008870

Printed in the United States of America
Mankato, MN
082022

ABOUT THE AUTHOR

Rachel Kehoe is a science writer and children's author. She has published several books and articles on science, technology, and climate change.

TABLE OF CONTENTS

CHAPTER 1

Farming Grows Up 5

CHAPTER 2

Climate in Danger 9

CHAPTER 3

Earth-Friendly Farming 15

THAT'S AMAZING!

Agroforestry 20

CHAPTER 4

Food for the Future 23

Focus on Improving Farming and Food Science • 30
Glossary • 31
To Learn More • 32
Index • 32

CHAPTER 1

FARMING GROWS UP

Near the heart of Newark, New Jersey, is a farm. But this farm doesn't rest on rolling green hills. It's in the middle of a city. The farm rises straight into the air.

Vertical farms grow food inside tall buildings. Vegetables such as spinach and lettuce grow in stacked shelves.

Baby kale grows at a vertical farm in Newark, New Jersey.

In vertical farms, plants often receive red and blue light. Those kinds of light help the plants grow.

Artificial light helps them grow. Recycled water **irrigates** the crops.

Computers control the levels of light, humidity, and temperature. As a result, the food can be grown year-round. Vertical farms are also less exposed to weather hazards. Floods, hurricanes, and droughts cannot wipe out the crops. Plus, growing plants indoors protects them from insects, pests, and weeds.

Vertical farming grows more food in less space. This system is vital in places with little farmland. It is also one of many solutions to help fight **climate change**.

GREENS IN THE SKY

The country of Singapore lies on a small island. But it is home to more than five million people. As of 2021, it grew only 7 percent of its food. The rest came from overseas. However, Singapore was working to make 30 percent of its own food by 2030. The country planned to shift to vertical farms.

CHAPTER 2

CLIMATE IN DANGER

Producing food is big business. And it is only getting bigger. As countries develop, people buy more meat, eggs, and dairy. These changes create serious problems. That's because agriculture is a leading cause of climate change.

Livestock pollute the air with **greenhouse gases**. Their digestive

Between the 1960s and the 2010s, the world's beef production more than doubled.

 Most deforestation of the Amazon rainforest happens because ranchers clear large areas to raise cattle.

systems and manure produce methane. The fertilizers used to grow their food produce nitrous oxide. These greenhouse gases trap the sun's heat in the atmosphere. They do so more powerfully than the carbon dioxide (CO_2) from vehicles and power plants does. These methane and nitrous oxide **emissions** contribute to climate change.

The problem is not limited to adding gases. People are also taking away Earth's ability to remove them. Trees and plants absorb CO_2 from the air. But forests are shrinking from **deforestation**.

THE BRAZIL NUT TREE

Deforestation threatens many plants and animals. One of them is the Brazil nut tree. It lives in the Amazon rainforest. All trees absorb CO_2. But the Brazil nut tree does it better than most. It helps keep Earth's temperature steady. However, this tree is at risk of dying out. More than 17 percent of the Amazon has already been destroyed.

Companies are clearing forests for farms and ranches. Clearing forests releases their stored carbon back into the air.

Deforestation harms natural habitats, too. Fewer plants and animals survive. Those areas lose their variety of life.

Not all food is equally responsible for climate change. Raising animals uses a lot of land. Livestock take up nearly 80 percent of all farmland. Only 20 percent is for crops. Beef and pork also provide fewer calories per acre compared to plants or chickens. They provide less protein per acre, too. This means an area of farmland can support more vegetarians than meat-eaters.

Unfortunately, approximately one-third of food is wasted. Some food is lost during transport. Huge amounts are thrown away. This wastes the water, soil, and land that helped make the food. It wastes the energy, too.

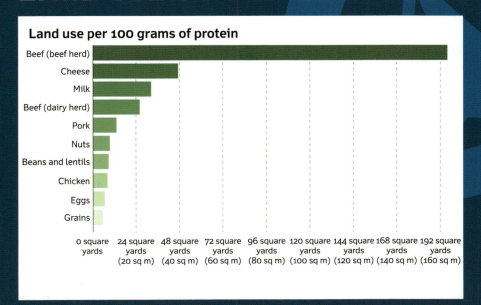

CHAPTER 3

EARTH-FRIENDLY FARMING

Many farming practices are good for the climate. One is regenerative farming. This kind of farming improves the health of soil. Healthy soil stores carbon. That helps slow climate change.

Crop rotation is one regenerative farming practice. Suppose a farmer grows carrots one year. Carrots need nitrogen

Farmers often use corn and bean plants in crop rotation.

to grow. The second year, the farmer grows peas and beans. Peas and beans add nitrogen to the soil. The third year, the soil has nitrogen again. It has the nutrients to support more carrots. By rotating crops, the soil can store carbon.

Zero tillage is another helpful regenerative method. Carbon is released when soil is disturbed. But farmers can grow crops without digging or plowing. Many use no-till planters. These tools make tiny holes in the ground. They plant the seeds directly into the holes. Then the tools cover the holes with soil. That way, farmers don't need to dig up the soil. This keeps carbon in the ground.

Regular tilling practices dig up much of the soil on a farm. They also reduce the soil's health.

Ranchers can also raise livestock in Earth-friendly ways. For example, ranches often have too many cows on a piece of land. The cows can cause **overgrazing**. Sometimes plants cannot recover. But ranchers can regularly rotate cows across grazing areas. This practice lets land rest. It increases the land's carbon storage.

In addition, farmers can use more **efficient** techniques. For instance, irrigation is needed in many places. Pumping the water requires a huge amount of energy. It is a major source of carbon emissions. Plus, irrigation often uses sprinklers. Sprinklers spray water all over a farm. As a result, the method wastes lots of water. But scientists have developed drip irrigation. In drip irrigation, machines deliver the exact amount of water that plants need. The water also goes straight to the roots. That way, there's much less wasted water.

Even with improved food production, waste would still be a problem. Causes of

Drip irrigation often uses hoses that drip the right amount of water exactly where the plants are growing.

food waste vary. In wealthier countries, consumers are the biggest food-wasters. In developing countries, most food loss occurs during storage. To help, scientists designed new storage bags. Each bag has three layers. A seal cuts off the oxygen supply. This gets rid of insects. Farmers can store food without it going bad.

THAT'S AMAZING!

AGROFORESTRY

Agroforestry combines planting trees with growing crops and raising livestock. This practice reduces deforestation. It cleans waterways and keeps soil healthy. Trees also provide shade. This prevents animals from overheating. Too much sun can also dry out the soil and burn leafy crops.

Plants such as cacao, vanilla, and coffee grow best in tree shade. In many countries, agroforestry is used to grow coffee plants. This practice has been used for hundreds of years. Shade-grown coffee makes a better product. It can be grown with less fertilizer. Trees also protect crops from wind and rain.

Agroforestry fights climate change, too. More trees mean more CO_2 gets soaked up from the air. Every year, agroforestry keeps 750 million

Coffee plants grow under the shade of trees in Ecuador.

tons (680 million metric tons) of CO_2 out of the atmosphere. Trees and their roots can store carbon for many years.

CHAPTER 4

FOOD FOR THE FUTURE

Wealthy countries often view food as easy to replace. For example, many people throw away food that's past its "best-before" date. But this label gives misleading information. Food past this date is often still safe to eat. For this reason, removing "best-before" dates can prevent food waste.

The amount of food wasted every year could feed billions of people.

Individuals can waste less food in other ways. They can plan meals more carefully. Then they can buy only what they need. After meals, people can store leftovers. Those leftovers can become new meals.

Farmers and consumers can **compost** more. Composting reduces food waste sent to landfills. This cuts methane emissions. Compost also returns what people have taken from Earth. Organic materials break down. They become a natural fertilizer that makes nutrient-rich soil. Less chemical fertilizer is needed.

People can also work to change what they eat. Eating more plants and less meat is better for the climate. A variety of

Sambar is a popular lentil and vegetable stew in South India. It has no meat or dairy and is high in protein.

diets already promote this. For example, Mediterranean diets are high in fruits, vegetables, and nuts. And people across India eat mainly rice, lentils, and stew. Both diets feature less meat and dairy.

Even so, some people struggle to switch eating habits. Scientists have developed other ways to cut meat consumption. Lab-grown meat uses fewer cows and less land. It starts off as tiny

SEAWEED FIGHTS COW BURPS

Cows' stomachs can digest grass. But that process forms a lot of methane. This gas comes out as burps. Scientists discovered that seaweed reduces cow methane. Farmers around the globe now mix it into cows' food. The animals burped much less. Some of the cows produced much less methane. But problems remain. There isn't enough seaweed to feed all of the world's cows. Farmers are looking for ways to grow more seaweed. It is an Earth-friendly way to cut livestock emissions.

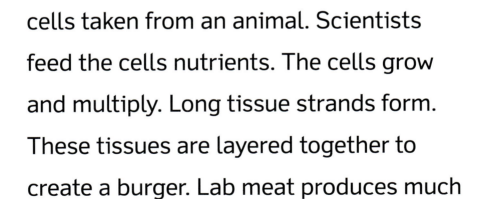

No animals are harmed or killed from producing lab meat.

cells taken from an animal. Scientists feed the cells nutrients. The cells grow and multiply. Long tissue strands form. These tissues are layered together to create a burger. Lab meat produces much lower greenhouse gas emissions than regular meat. But as of the early 2020s, it was still expensive to make. Scientists were working to make lab meat cheaper.

Plant-based proteins produce even fewer emissions. They don't use any animal products. Instead, soy, flours, and oils are added to plant protein. These ingredients recreate the taste, texture, and appearance of meat. Several restaurants gave customers both a meat burger and a plant-based burger. Many customers couldn't taste the difference.

Farming is one of the world's most important industries. Currently, it is taking a toll on the environment. But that doesn't have to happen. Many farming practices produce food without draining resources. They reduce greenhouse gases. By protecting Earth, we can make healthy food for years to come.

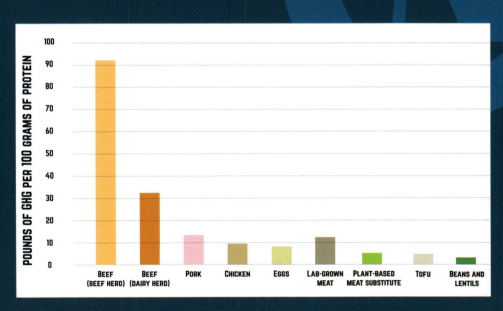

EMISSIONS FROM PROTEIN

This chart shows the average greenhouse gas (GHG) emissions per 100 grams of protein for different foods.

FOCUS ON
IMPROVING FARMING AND FOOD SCIENCE

Write your answers on a separate piece of paper.

1. Write a paragraph describing the main ideas of Chapter 4.

2. Have you ever tried plant-based meat? If so, what did you think? If not, would you like to?

3. What is an example of a regenerative farming practice?
   - **A.** overgrazing
   - **B.** plant-based meat
   - **C.** crop rotation

4. What will happen if Earth experiences more deforestation?
   - **A.** Greenhouse gas emissions will decrease.
   - **B.** Greenhouse gas emissions will increase.
   - **C.** Greenhouse gas emissions will stay the same.

Answer key on page 32.

GLOSSARY

climate change
A human-caused global crisis involving long-term changes in Earth's temperature and weather patterns.

compost
To cause food to break down and turn into fertilizer.

deforestation
The removal of the trees in a forest, usually by cutting or burning.

efficient
Accomplishing as much as possible with as little effort or as few resources as possible.

emissions
Chemicals or substances that are released into the air, especially ones that harm the environment.

greenhouse gases
Gases that trap heat in Earth's atmosphere, causing climate change.

irrigates
Waters crops though human-made means, such as pipes.

overgrazing
When farm animals eat large numbers of plants in a certain area, harming those plants' ability to regrow.

TO LEARN MORE

BOOKS

Burling, Alexis. *Turning Poop into Power*. Minneapolis: Abdo Publishing, 2020.

Cornell, Kari. *Dig In!: 12 Easy Gardening Projects Using Kitchen Scraps*. Minneapolis: Lerner Publications, 2018.

Gitlin, Martin. *Smart Farming*. Ann Arbor, MI: Cherry Lake Publishing, 2021.

NOTE TO EDUCATORS

Visit **www.focusreaders.com** to find lesson plans, activities, links, and other resources related to this title.

INDEX

agroforestry, 20–21

beef, 12–13, 29
Brazil nut tree, 11

chicken, 12–13, 29
composting, 24
crop rotation, 15–16

deforestation, 11–12, 20
drip irrigation, 18

food waste, 13, 18–19, 23–24

India, 25

lab-grown meat, 26–29
livestock, 9, 12, 17, 20, 26

Mediterranean diets, 25

Newark, New Jersey, 5

overgrazing, 17

plant-based meat, 28–29
pork, 12–13, 29
protein, 12–13, 28–29

regenerative farming, 15–16

Singapore, 7

vertical farms, 5–7

zero tillage, 16

Answer Key: 1. Answers will vary; **2.** Answers will vary; **3.** C; **4.** B